To Save a Life

Table of Contents

Dedication's page

This little book is dedicated to all of the firefighters around the world that put their lives on the line so that some other person may live after a fire or some other tragic event.

I would like to offer a sincere "Thank you" to the producer that makes an audio book from this little book.

It was 6 a.m. when the alarm went off at the fire chief's home.

He crawled out of the bed quickly.

This was a habit that was hard to break.

He knew that the equipment had to be checked before the little fire fighters could go out and save the lives of the community.

The fire chief arrived at the fire station and he began to make sure that everything was stocked and the equipment was working properly.

The fire chief's name was Claude.

Claude checked the fire extinguishers first.

The fire extinguishers were very important. Normally they were not used unless the fire was small.

The "ABC" fire extinguisher was the best out of all of the fire extinguishers because it could be used for every type of small fire.

Next, Claude checked all of the little fire ladders on the fire truck.

He wanted to make sure that the little firemen were safe when they went on a fire run in the community.

His staff was very important to him.

Next, the little fire chief checked all of the fire hoses.

He wanted to be sure that all of the hoses were in good working condition before any fire run had to take place.

Claude tapped the fire hoses one at a time.

He had to make sure that everything worked properly.

Claude loved his job.

Next, he began to look at all of the firemen's gear and the fire truck itself.

He wanted to make extra sure that all of his staff would be safe and secure.

Next, Claude began to check the fire truck.

He tooted the horn on the little truck and then he checked all of the seats.

Claude smiled as he walked into the fire station then.

He was sure that his staff would be safe and secure now.

Just as the little fire chief walked inside the fire station, the alarm began to ring.

"Duty calls" he said to all of his staff.

All of the little firemen began to get up out of their beds very quickly.

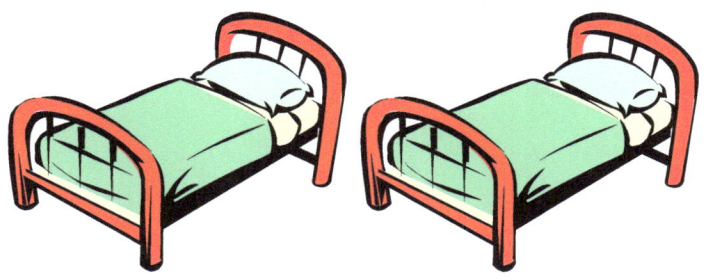

The firemen knew that it was time to work.

"Time to go meet Sparky" they all said.

"He can be a mean little booger" one firemen said to another.

"I know that's right" the other little firefighter replied.

They all began to get dressed.

Next, they all slid down the fire pole to get on their assigned fire truck.

They knew that "Sparky" could be everywhere and they also knew what sort of damage that he was capable of.

The little firefighters had nicknamed any fire "Sparky".

The dispatcher told all of them that "Sparky" had been busy over the last couple of minutes.

She told them that "Sparky" had set a building on fire.

Next, she told them that "Sparky" had set a couple of logs on fire in the woods.

Then she told the little firefighters that "Sparky" had also set a small house on fire as well.

The little firefighters looked very upset.

They knew how dangerous "Sparky" could be.

Claude and the dispatcher told one group of firefighters to go and take care of the building that "Sparky" had caught on fire.

They all nodded in Claude's direction and did as they were instructed.

They arrived to find that the building was full of smoke and "Sparky" had spread over one side of the building already.

The little firefighters quickly got out of the truck and began to go immediately to work.

Roger immediately noticed the small boy waving his hands in the air and he was pleading for help.

The little boy noticed the fire truck and he began to calm down just a little.

Roger placed the fire ladder at the side of the building and began to make his way up the building to the small child.

"It's all right little guy" Roger said.

"I am here now" he said again to the small child.

"Just try and stay calm" Roger replied once more.

The little boy nodded his head in agreement.

Roger placed his arms around the small boy and slowly pulled him to safety and placed him on the ladder with him.

The little boy threw his arms around Roger's neck immediately.

"Thank you" the little boy replied.

"You are very welcome" Roger exclaimed.

"I was so scared" the little boy said again.

"I know son but you are safe now" Roger said.

The little boy just smiled at Roger then.

This made Roger's day.

He was also so happy when he could save a life.

This made his job meaningful and Roger knew that he had a purpose in life.

The next fire unit was sent to the small house that "Sparky" had caught on fire.

The firemen arrived and they saw "Sparky" close up then.

Sparky was laughing at all of them.

"Put me out if you can, Mr. Fireman" Sparky said to all of them.

All of the firemen just smiled at him.

"We sure will" they all said in unison.

They brought out their ladders and fire hoses and began to put Sparky out.

The firemen aimed all of the hoses at Sparky then.

Sparky tried to run away so that he could start another fire elsewhere but all of the firemen cornered him at the house.

They were going to make sure that he didn't get to spread anywhere else in town that day.

The firemen smiled as Sparky began to fade away from the small house that was on fire.

They knew that they had defeated him that day.

All of the firemen felt good then.

Thankfully, no one was at home when "Sparky" paid the house a visit.

The last unit arrived in the woods just in time.

"Sparky" had set a couple of logs on fire.

The little firemen just smiled again at each other.

They just could not believe some of the damage that "Sparky" was actually capable of doing in just a small amount of time.

They knew that if they had not arrived when they had that "Sparky" would have set the entire woodlands on fire.

The little firemen knew what type of damage that could have been caused if "Sparky" had reached the woods.

As the fire trucks arrived back at the fire station, they all patted each other on the back for a job well done.

They absolutely loved their jobs.

All of the little firemen were always happy when they could save a life, whether it be a human life, animal life or someone's property.

The little firemen always give back to their community.

It is just their human nature.

So, if you see a fire fighter out somewhere where you are, give them a hug and/or offer them a sincere "Thank you" for the community service

they perform that keeps all of us safe and secure on a daily basis.

You should always make them feel appreciated since they put their lives on the line to save yours!

This will make their job ever more meaningful and put a smile on their face.

The End

To Save a Life is about all of the little fire fighters that put their lives on the line to save ours. This little book gives three examples of some common hazards that firemen face on a daily basis and how they save people's lives. What examples does this book explore? Do you appreciate firemen? Have you hugged a fireman lately? Read on a find out for yourself!!!

Misty Lynn Wesley has a diversified career portfolio in the medical, legal, fashion and insurance industries. She is an avid blogger for Examiner.com and she sometimes writes for CBS Local out of St. Paul, Minnesota and Believe.com She has also published four books with Publish America and several on Amazon. She and her chosen producers have made several audio books as well. So if you have time, check out the rest of the books and audio books. God bless and enjoy!

www.ingramcontent.com/pod-product-compliance
Lightning Source LLC
Chambersburg PA
CBHW050925290526
45792CB00002B/892